Bright Waters, Shining Tides

Sunrise behind Squibnocket Point oil on linen 24 x 40 inches 1979

Bright Waters, Shining Tides

REFLECTIONS ON A LIFETIME OF FISHING

Paintings and essays by

KIB BRAMHALL

VINEYARD STORIES, EDGARTOWN, MASSACHUSETTS

To Tess

For her loving patience with my compulsions and her encouragement to put this volume together.

Volume Copyright ©2011 by Kib Bramhall

Published by

VINEYARD STORIES

RR 1, Box 65-B9

Edgartown, MA 02539

508 221 2338

www.vineyardstories.com

ISBN 978-0-9827146-6-9
Library of Congress Control Number: 2011926700

Book Design: Alley Moore

With appreciation to both *Salt Water Sportsman* and
Martha's Vineyard Magazine.

Thanks to my daughter Nina Bramhall for
photographing many of the paintings for this book.

Back cover photograph © Mark Alan Lovewell 2011

Printed in Canada

Contents

Introduction

I was raised in a family fishing contest in the late 1930s in Mantoloking on the New Jersey coast, where my family spent the summers and where my grandfather, Jacques Bramhall, built a house right on the primary dune. It was known as Upsandunes. It contained a large tackle room that was the command center of a season-long surf fishing contest whose participants included three aunts, two uncles, my father, and grandfather. They were assigned their own areas of the room to keep rods, reels, boots, slickers, tin squids, hooks, sinkers, and other gear, and there were large wooden revolving spools on which the Cuttyhunk linen fishing lines were dried after being washed in freshwater following each day's use. There was a blackboard on which daily, weekly, monthly, and seasonal scores were kept for the largest striped bass, bluefish, weakfish, croaker, kingfish, and flounder. The aroma was of sea mist and oilskins, and I grew up there and on the beach, a willing and devout student of a pastime that I would practice into the next century.

Eventually I graduated from being a mere mascot and learned how to take apart and clean a variety of revolving spool reels made by such venerable firms as Penn, Vom Hofe, and Ocean City. And how to reverse the guides on Calcutta bamboo rods to counter the curve they acquired from prolonged use. And how to rub block tin squids with wet beach sand until they took on just the right shine to imitate the glimmer of baitfish. And how to bait hooks with clams, sand crabs, mussels, and squid. And all the while it became increasingly apparent to me that life's holy grail was the search to become a successful surf fisherman, particularly for striped bass. My first bible was *Fishing the Surf* by Raymond R. Camp, who wrote the daily "Wood, Field and Stream" column for the *New York Times*.

My father and grandfather fishing at Mantoloking, 1938.

Upsandunes, 1938

Published in 1941 it was touted as the first book of any kind devoted to the sport of surf fishing. My first-edition copy, which is inscribed "To J. Bramhall—tight lines—Ray Camp", is among my prized possessions.

My first bass is indelibly etched in my mind. It was a sparkling summer day in 1940. I was seven and had learned to cast respectably. I had my own outfit, and I set off down the beach with it to join my father, Keasbey, and grandfather, who were bait fishing half a mile away in a hole by the old Dunes Hotel. When I was nearly there a flock of terns began diving into the white water of tumbling surf, and an angel whispered in my ear that this would be a good place to make a cast with the Ed's #7 block tin squid that was attached to my line. Something grabbed it the instant it hit the water—my first connection to a mysterious and powerful sea creature. To this day I can still feel the awe and excitement and, yes, fright of that take. It was a striper, not very large, but incredibly beautiful and vastly important because it was the first. There was such a rush of pride and excitement when I beached it that I could have walked on the clouds. My spirit and the water and the fish were bonded forever in that moment.

The family fishing contest ran in abbreviated form during World War II, with my father and uncles serving in the armed forces, and the beach at Mantoloking often yielding grim evidence of the torpedoed freighters and tankers we could sometimes see burning offshore at night. There was a Coast Guard station a hundred yards from our house, where I was befriended and fed by the crew, who were intensely interested in and talked incessantly about my beautiful aunts, often with words that I did not understand. There were plenty of fish in the surf, and we caught our share, but the excitement and tension of the war diminished the prime importance that fishing had played until then. The day after it ended— VJ Day plus one—my mother took me on a trip that would alter the rest of my life.

Her parents were spending the summer on Martha's Vineyard, and we set out to visit them, taking the Cape Codder train from Grand Central Station in New York to Woods Hole, where we would board the ferry. The streets of New York were littered with confetti and other leftovers of an uproarious victory celebration, and the train crew was still partying. By the time we reached Providence they were too drunk to continue; so we disembarked and shared a cab to Woods Hole, where we found that the ferry crew was similarly disabled. My mother—nothing if not determined—repaired to a bar stool at the

Wasque oil on paper 8 1/2 x 11 inches 1957

*This painting, depicting the author's brother and father, was
his first sale at the Old Sculpin Gallery in Edgartown in 1957.*

Captain Kidd Restaurant, and in the wink of an eye had convinced a fisherman to take us across the sound on his boat. And so it was on August 15, 1945, at the age of twelve that I first set foot on the island that would be a pivotal part of my life and eventually my home. The Chamber of Commerce called it an island surrounded by striped bass.

Starting in 1947 my parents became summer renters in Edgartown. My father's parents had died, Upsandunes had been sold, and the Vineyard was now the focus of our summer life. It was a far different place back then. The waterfront streets in downtown Edgartown were unpaved, there was a blacksmith shop and a fish market near the yacht club, and Manuel Schwartz was still making catboats in the building that now houses the Old Sculpin art gallery. "Up Island" was only a rumor to most summer people, and electricity and phones were just coming to North Road in Chilmark and West Tisbury. The Island as a summer resort had been discovered by only a prescient few, and day trippers had not been invented yet.

There were only a handful of surfcasters, and my father, brother David, and I usually had the famed fishing rip at Wasque Point on Chappaquiddick to ourselves. We fished by the clock, not by the tides, because my father believed that there was a time and a place for everything, and the time for fishing was between lunch and his evening cocktails. Reached by a winding, rugged dirt road that few cared to traverse, Wasque seemed like an undiscovered frontier where we caught striped bass, bluefish, and weakfish on block tin Ferron jigs, split bamboo rods, and Penn Surfmaster reels. Sturgeon were also plentiful off Wasque, leaping from the water like elevators rising from the deep and then falling back with gigantic splashes, and we witnessed Sheila Rice land and release an estimated eighty-pounder that she had foul hooked. Years later, in 1959, I was privileged to be part of The Trustees of Reservations successful fund-raising effort to buy and preserve forever this magical spot.

When my father was back in New York working on Wall Street, I would make the trip to

At Muskegut in 1947 on Steve Gentle's Seabee amphibian.

Wasque by bicycle or else bike to South Beach and walk to Katama Opening. That's when I got lucky and met my first Island mentors, Tony Gaspar, Warren Norton, and Preston Luce, who were nice enough to pick up a summer kid and take him fishing time and again in their Jeep and impart lots of local wisdom that would have taken years to learn on my own. In a similar way I also met Tom Osborne, who invited me to fly with him and a friend to Muskeget Island on Steve Gentle's Seabee amphibian for an overnight bass fishing trip. It was a hard sell to persuade my mother to agree, but in the end she let me go. We took off from the grass strip at the Katama airport and landed in a sheltered bay on that sandy atoll near Nantucket. After schlepping our gear to a ramshackle, gull-infested shack known as Camp Roccus Lineatus, we cast Ferrons along the north shore of the island and ran smack into a big school of eighteen- to twenty-five-pound stripers. I had never caught bass of that size and was awed by their power. In my inexperience I

1965 charcoal illustration for Salt Water Sportsman.

lost several due to straightened hooks and broken lines. It was 1947, and I was fourteen and about to go away to boarding school.

My early enthusiasm for fishing never left me. After graduating from college and a stint in the army, I took a job at *Salt Water Sportsman*, a monthly magazine devoted to saltwater sport fishing, and my wife Tess and I moved to the Boston area, where we raised a family of three wonderful children. My title at *SWS* was advertising director, but in reality I did

everything except sweep the floor. My duties included selling and designing ads, representing the magazine at sportsmen's and boat shows, proofreading and helping lay out each issue, field testing fishing equipment, writing and illustrating feature articles, photography, and public relations. I also traveled to nearby and far fishing areas, often with the magazine's famed editor, Frank Woolner, a World War II veteran who was a legend and a hero in the outdoor writing world. He and the magazine's publisher, Hal Lyman, had coauthored *The Complete Book of Striped Bass Fishing,* which was a bible to thousands of anglers, including myself. It was a dream job, and I stayed at it for eighteen years from 1956 until 1973, when I resigned from the magazine to pursue a full-time career as an artist.

There were many fishing highlights along the way, such as catching forty-pound stripers at Provincetown with Frank Woolner while living in his iconic, camouflaged Massachusetts Beach Buggy Association #13 van, and hanging out with his friends in the "Worcester gang" of tremendously talented anglers including Arnold Laine, Charlie Whitney, David and Rosa Webb, and Jack and Kay Townsend. In 1960 Kay shattered the women's world record for striped bass with a sixty-three-and-a-half-pounder, only to be beaten less than an hour later when her friend Rosa boated a sixty-four-and-a-half-pounder in the same stretch of P'town water! Both fish were taken live lining mackerel from tin boats launched in the surf, and I plagiarized the tin boat idea and believe that I was the first to launch one from the beaches of Martha's Vineyard. I piloted nine-, twelve-, and fourteen-footers all around the Island and as far away as Cuttyhunk and Nomans, nearby islands off the Vineyard's coast, and in 1967 caught the biggest bass in the boat division on the Martha's Vineyard Striped Bass and Bluefish Derby from my nine-footer. To this day my boats are named "Tin Boat" whether they are made from aluminum or fiberglass.

Woolner was indirectly responsible for my personal best striper, a sixty-pounder on June 17, 1959. A California lure manufacturer named John Perkins had asked us to show him what East Coast striped bass fishing was all about, and we decided to take him to Cuttyhunk on a charter trip with legendary skipper Bob Smith.

We spent the afternoon in Smith's kitchen drinking Scotch and telling fish stories as a building northeaster splattered rain against the windows. By the time we finished dinner at the Allen House, the wind was gusting to forty and the rain was coming down in sheets. All the other charter skippers cancelled their trips, but not

The author's sixty-pounder caught on Captain Bob Smith's Susan B *on June 19, 1959.*

Smith, who said conditions would be perfect at one of his hot spots. Perkins couldn't believe we were going out into that maelstrom and thought we were kidding until Smith's *Susan B* hit the rip at Canapissit at full throttle and went airborne

into Vineyard Sound. Then we pounded our way to Quick's Hole, where there was a lee and a surging east tide rip full of big bass. Woolner and Perkins handled the trolling rods, wire line outfits rigged with Smith's doctored Russellures, while I waited my turn amid a growing pile of large stripers that Smith gaffed aboard while faultlessly steering the boat with the tiller held between his butt cheeks. After landing another forty-pounder, Frank took pity on me and offered me his seat. I had stripped off no more than fifty feet of line when the big one inhaled my lure and made five long runs before succumbing to Smith's deadly gaff. It was a beautifully proportioned bass, fifty-two inches long with a girth of thirty-one inches and a weight of exactly sixty pounds on the Cuttyhunk scale.

Through the 1960s and '70s my passion for fishing matured and began to cool, replaced by the desire and need to make a career as a painter. And then in the late '70s and early '80s, just when my painting career was taking off with solo shows at a New York gallery, a new angling challenge emerged: saltwater fly fishing. I had to reinvent myself, learning fly fishing basics with Vineyard mentors like Nelson Bryant, Arthur Silvia, and Bruce Pratt and traveling to Florida to attend clinics run by such luminaries as Lefty Kreh, Al McLane, Flip Pallot, Mark Sosin, and Chico Fernandez. It was new and demanding, and there was a terrific adrenaline rush when it all came together.

I regained my fishing intensity and traveled to the Bahamas, the Florida Keys, Mexico, Central America, Scotland, and Iceland with my fly rods. I even set a couple of fly rod world records for striped bass and Atlantic bonito. I taught myself to cast equally well with either my right or left arm. I became a fly rod purist, foregoing all the old angling disciplines that had given me such pleasure for so long.

That mind-set lasted for about twenty years, and then my outlook changed once again when I realized how much I missed the old stuff. I went back to casting plugs, bucktails, jigs, soft plastic lures, and eels, and to trolling tubes and spoons and whatever else worked. Fly fishing became only one aspect of my angling persona, not the whole thing,

As I write this in 2011, I have been saltwater fishing for more than seventy years and have been witness to the huge changes that have adversely affected our oceans and nearly all of its inhabitants in the late twentieth and early twenty-first centuries. Pollution, overfishing, population growth, and technology have combined to put relentless pressure on most fish species and threatened to wipe out some of them. At the same time, fishing equipment has improved exponentially, while boats and their electronics are products of the space age.

And yet, for me, there remains the fundamental challenge and thrill that hooked me when I caught that first striper in 1940 at age seven: the quest to make a connection with mysterious, beautiful inhabitants of the ocean from which we sprang and to understand the tides and winds and weather that govern their lives and by extension my own. ◆

The Mad Russian

A night for bass.

The rising tide laps softly against a rock-strewn beach, while beyond the swelling breakers the ocean is rippled by a gentle onshore breeze. The pale glow of a waning moon filters through the misty dark, punctuated by mysterious cloud shapes that drift across the sky like apparitions. Baitfish rustle nervously in the wash of a deep hole formed by the movement of tides and waves through a break in the offshore sandbar.

A mile to the west and a half mile off the beach, a pod of large stripers moves out of a dying tide rip, slowly following the current, heading toward the surf.

At the same moment, four miles inland, a wraithlike figure emerges from the doorway of a shingled cottage and ghosts through the darkness to a Jeep concealed behind nearby foliage. It has already been loaded with heavy-duty surf tackle, an assortment of customized lures with hooks filed to pinpoint sharpness, waders, gaff, billy, a container of live eels, and perhaps some lobster meat for gourmet bass bait. The engine coughs, shattering the night's stillness.

Morning Has Broken oil on linen 36 x 50 inches 1979

Sergei de Somov, the famed Mad Russian of the Northeast striper coast, moves toward another rendezvous with his prey.

It is the hour before dawn, and the pod of bass is moving faster now, almost with a sense of urgency. As they reach the break in the offshore bar, several of the fish swim through into the deep hole, warily at first and then with a surge. These forerunners move into the wash of the surf, and the rest follow. Thousands of baitfish panic as big stripers move in for the kill.

Minutes earlier a blacked-out Jeep had coasted to a stop behind a dune overlooking this hole. The beach is deserted except for the figure moving from the vehicle toward the surf.

It is no accident or stroke of luck that de Somov has come to this particular stretch of beach at a magic hour when trophy bass have arrived for a predawn breakfast. His trip had been planned with scientific precision that took into account many factors: wind direction on that day and several days previous; tidal stage and direction of flow; the amount of bait along this beach and in adjacent waters; recent and past patterns of striper movement and behavior in this area; water conditions, including clarity, temperature, and roughness; the hour itself. All these things had been observed and weighed with penetrating Russian logic and an answer arrived at.

De Somov's eyes sparkle, and a wide grin creases his face. He knows his decision was right. Baitfish are being driven high onto the beach by the marauding bass, and the swirls of big fish can be seen in the eerie moon mist. The long surf rod is swept back to make the first cast—but *wait!*

Headlights bob over the horizon half a mile down the beach. A vehicle has turned off the access road onto the sand and is driving toward him. De Somov swiftly retraces his steps to the concealment of the dune and watches as it stops a couple of hundred yards away. Dim figures emerge, spread out, and start probing the surf. False dawn has nearly arrived, and de Somov *might be seen* if he went back to those bass. He

Below the Tidemark oil on linen 32 x 46 inches 1982

has only one alternative, and he takes it without hesitation. The rod is racked, the engine coughs, and with lights still extinguished he vanishes down the beach.

Has this expedition been a maddening failure? Not completely. Not to the Mad Russian. It was galling, of course, that such careful plans had to be abandoned at the very moment of consummation, but this was balanced by his success at having avoided detection. It had been a close call, but in the end no one had caught so much as a glimpse of him. Those other anglers had been unaware of his nearby presence. He had remained a virtual phantom of the surf.

Well, it might have happened that way, and then again maybe it didn't. There is no way of knowing, because it was impossible to penetrate the closely guarded secrecy that cloaked the Mad Russian's surf fishing trips—secrecy that helped make this eccentric, brilliant fisherman a legend in his own time.

Although de Somov's methods, his nocturnal wanderings on the striper coast, and his battles with outsized stripers were shrouded in mystery, his exploits were not. For the past two decades he had racked up eye-popping catches on the beaches of Long Island and New Jersey, as well as on the Vineyard. And that is what made him such a compelling subject of speculation among the hard-core fraternity of surfmen. The courtly gentleman with the foreign accent kept showing up with big stripers, and no one knew exactly how, when, or where he caught them.

Perhaps his most astounding accomplishments occurred on Martha's Vineyard during the Island's annual striped bass and bluefish derbies. These monthlong autumn contests attract thousands of participants, including many of the most skilled surf fishermen on the Northeast coast. For three consecutive years—in 1963, 1964, and 1965—de Somov took on all competitors and won top honors for the largest striper with fish of fifty-two pounds, thirteen ounces; fifty-four pounds, fourteen ounces; and forty-nine pounds, ten ounces. No one else has matched that achievement in the contest's venerable history.

Afternoon Light oil on linen 24 x 36 inches 1986

Sergei de Somov and the author in 1966. Both were inducted into the Derby Hall of Fame when it was first established in 1999.

Sergei de Somov was born on Christmas morning 1896 in St. Petersburg, Russia. His father was in the diplomatic service, and Sergei gained working knowledge of eight languages during his cosmopolitan upbringing. After graduating from college he became a member of Her Majesty's Imperial Lancers and rose to the rank of major. He immigrated to the United States in 1923 and settled in New York City, where he taught school, then worked on Wall Street, moved to the Edison Company, and finally joined the National Broadcasting Company in 1929, where he worked for the next nineteen years.

The salt air and sea beckoned, and in the early 1930s Sergei moved to Long Island, where he joined the East End Surf Fishing Club. From that time forward, the angling world began hearing colorful tales of piscatorial prowess, of strange homemade lures, of occult nocturnal fishing trips, of an elusive foreign gentleman who consistently beached big striped bass—always while fishing alone.

The beginnings of Sergei's fishing career were as exotic as his methods were bizarre. In 1911, when he was fifteen years old, his father introduced him to the fine art of angling on the Han-Gahn River in Korea, where the elder de Somov was stationed as a representative of his country's government. The quarry? Korean fahak, or blowfish. The tackle? Spinning, decades before it made its appearance in this country.

In spite of having been weaned on spinning tackle, de Somov had no love for it when I knew him in the 1950s and '60s on the Vineyard. A surf spinning outfit was a "yo-yo" rig as far as he was concerned, perfectly okay for small fish, but not adequate for the trophy bass that were his quarry. For these he used heavy-duty conventional tackle: rods with stiff backbone and revolving spool reels filled with a minimum forty-five-pound-test Dacron braid tied directly to his lures. When he thought there was a chance for a record striper, he upgraded to his "man-killer" rig—a herculean rod mounting an oversize reel spooled with eighty-pound-test. He was only interested in catching big bass. Schoolies were "nuisance fish."

He made many of his own lures, but he caught one of his Vineyard Derby winners on a plug that he borrowed from me. It was a big swimming plug called the Sea Serpent, which was armed with two large, extra-strong single hooks. It was made in Germany and designed to catch tuna on the North African coast. I saw it in a tackle store in Paris and brought it back to the Vineyard to use on striped bass. I showed it to Sergei, who said "Ah, Kib, that is a very serious plug. May I borrow it?" Of course I loaned it to him, and he gave me a photo of his winning bass with it in its mouth. The plug itself, however, I never saw again.

Sergei was seventy years old when I got to know him in 1963. He was of medium height and appeared slight in physique, and I wondered how he could wield such heavy tackle until we shook hands. He had a grip like a professional football player. He kept himself in superb physical condition, walking countless miles along the beach, observing water and topographical

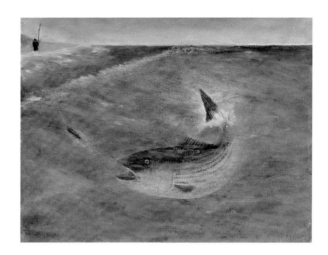

Raising a Bass oil on paper 9 x 12 inches 1958

conditions every step of the way. He tested water temperatures and took note of holes and hidden bars, of water clarity, of baitfish, of gull behavior, and then sifted and stored the data with scientific thoroughness. When he decided—and the decision was never casual—that all indications pointed favorably to the likelihood of big stripers visiting a certain stretch of surf, only then did he make plans to be there, too. And, of course, such plans were always contingent upon his being able to fish alone and unobserved, except for his wife,

Louise, who was an excellent angler in her own right, and with whom he conversed in French, Russian, and English—all in the same sentence.

The Mad Russian was a topic of conversation wherever surfmen gathered on the Northeast striper coast. His skill at beaching big bass would, by itself, have been enough to ensure his fame. The added elements of secrecy and continental politesse enhanced it tenfold. Many regarded him with awe akin to that commanded by the ancient deities. Others simply respected him. A jealous few protested that his skills were no more than ordinary, and that his elusive tactics were merely designed to mask the fact. But there is no disputing that he was and remains a legend. He added an aura of mystique to a sport that too many of us allow to enter the realm of the prosaic, and he brought a touch of poetry to the world of the high surf. It was a better place because of it. Sergei was inducted into the Derby Hall of Fame in 1999. ◆

This is an amended version of "Phantom in the Surf,"
published in the Salt Water Sportsman *(March 1967).*

The Dunes of July oil on linen 36 x 50 inches 1982

The World of the Night Surf

Anyone who has ever hooked a striped bass while the burst of a new day's dawn tints the sea will tell you that it is a soul-inspiring experience. So will the angler who has seen a bass cutting powerfully through a sea-green wave just before it crumbles into a frothy comber. Poetry and thousands of words of prose have been inspired by the visual beauty of the big blue-ceilinged arena where anglers do battle with bass in emerald seas. There's no doubt about it: daylight surf fishing for stripers is one of the most rewarding forms of fishing.

Me, I prefer fishing in the dead of night when it's so black you can't see your hand three inches in front of your face.

To the unappreciative, nothing seems quite so melancholy as the fisherman who sacrifices after-dinner card games, TV, sleep, and other civilized nighttime activities to go stumbling around the beach, casting into the dark, trying to catch a fish that probably isn't there in the first place—and which couldn't be seen if it was! "Besides," reasoned my father, "it's unsporting to catch fish in the middle of the night because they're half asleep and don't know what they're doing."

To its devotees, on the other hand, night surf fishing is more challenging and more rewarding than its daylight counterpart. It produces more

Night Fishing oil sketch on canvas paper 7 x 9 inches 1958

Black Cloud Sunset oil on linen 24 x 36 inches 2007

stripers. And bigger ones. Its aesthetics are taken from an altogether different frame of reference, and they are intensely poignant.

The prime raison d'être for nighttime bassing is that it is the most productive time. Stripers are primarily nocturnal feeders and aren't half asleep during the hours of darkness. They're predators looking for a meal. One's chances of enticing them to take a lure or bait are at their peak after the sun has set and before it comes up again.

This is particularly true in the case of surf fishing. Stripers, particularly during the summer months, tend to hang offshore in deeper, cooler, more protected waters during the hours of daylight. When darkness pervades the scene, they move inshore, looking for smaller baitfish that have sought shoal-water safety from the marauders of the deep. And they often move all the way in, right into the wash and undertow, so close that you could touch them with the tip of your rod if you knew they were there.

One thing that night fishermen have in common with each other is an unusually keen development of three of the five basic senses: hearing, sight, and touch. Many seasoned anglers also use their sense of smell to detect bass (the scent is sweet, almost chemical in nature and somewhat like thyme), but the striper-sensitive nose is employed similarly during daylight or dark. An angler who is a regular at the nighttime shift will as a rule possess a keenness of hearing usually developed only by the blind. He will be able to hear the slap of a striper's tail a hundred yards down the beach and distinguish it from a similar noise made by an eel. He will be able to hear, when the surf is quiet, the slightest pitter-patter of baitfish nervously rustling the water's surface, and he will be able to cast to the disturbance with sound as his only guide. He will be able to tell what size bass are breaking water, and by the sound he will know if they are feeding or simply rolling on the surface at play.

One reason he develops a blind man's keenness of hearing, of course, is that he operates in a world of darkness which at times is absolutely opaque, and at other times only faintly lighted by the moon and stars or ambient light from the horizon. Nevertheless, eyesight plays an important role, and night vision is the second basic sense developed to an unusually high degree by nocturnal surfmen.

There are nights when it is so dark that one might as well be blindfolded, and these are usually the nights when fishing is best. Such opacity is exceptional, however. There is usually some light, and the experienced angler's eyes are attuned to see and recognize forms and movements that would be invisible or meaningless to the neophyte. The swirl of a bass, for instance, disturbs the sea's surface in a way that can be spotted by the after-hours angler if there is only the faintest light. A fish that actually breaks the surface and splashes is even more easily seen (and heard). When there is phosphorus in the water, a quickly moving bass will leave a distinctive trail of "fire" in his wake. The looming form of an approaching wave will reveal whether it will break harmlessly or whether you'd better get out of its path, and the broken surface of water on a bar will show where it is safe to wade. Finally, when a hooked fish is dogging somewhere out in the black sea, his whereabouts can be determined by focusing on the line etched against a clear sky. On an opaque night when this is impossible, it is surprisingly difficult to determine just where your quarry is. This makes it very hard to land him.

The third basic sense which is developed to an extraordinary degree by after-hours surfmen is touch. The tugging of current against a lure or fly line reveals valuable information about the water being fished. A sudden letup in the tugging means that a wave has overtaken your offering and the retrieve should be speeded up until slack line is regained. When a striper slaps a rigged eel, the experienced basser stops his retrieve, recognizing the difference between the feel of such a slap and an actual hit. Anglers who refuse to use artificial light unless absolutely necessary can change flies or lures by touch alone. They periodically feel line and leader for evidence of abrasion, and similarly check snaps to be sure they are closed. On those ink-black nights when almost nothing is visible to even the most highly trained eye, one relies on feel to determine where a hooked fish is, when he is ready to be brought ashore, and when a breaking wave will help ease him through the surf.

Hearing, vision, and touch—senses that are developed to an acute degree by the successful night fishermen, and which all come into play in appreciating the occult aesthetics of the game. There can be visual beauty, yes. A million twinkling stars in a blue-black canopy create an awe-inspiring setting, and one of the most striking sights I have ever seen was a bass that hit a surface plug and leaped clear of the water perfectly silhouetted against a full autumn moon just rising above the horizon. But the real aesthetic wonder of casting into the vast blackness of the sea in the dead of night is the great sense of mystery. You cast into the unknown, senses keyed to the straining point trying to fathom what may be at the other end. Strong men tremble when, somewhere out there,

Night Visitor oil on paper 9 x 15 inches 1978

something grabs hold and rips line off the spool. At that moment you are locked in an intensely personal battle with an unknown adversary. There is nothing but the blackness of the night and the creature you have hooked. No scenery, no distractions, nothing. You are in an inky void with tackle strained by an adversary you cannot see. To the devotees of the dark, this is the moment that pales any daytime angling experience.

That strange clan who come to life after the sun has set and haunt the beaches in nocturnal blackness may not be as remote as you believe. Join them just once, and you too may be bitten by the allure and mystery of night-shrouded seas, by the electric excitement of battling an unseen adversary in opaque blackness. Against your will you could become a member of this race apart and forever more be cursed with the need to search out striped bass in the unearthly world of the night surf. ◆

This is an amended version of an article that appeared in Salt Water Sportsman *(1962).*

Magic Wands

Fly rods are the magic wands of sport fishing. They can transcend their designated role in the fishing tackle spectrum and become instruments of an art form in which the practitioner paints graceful loops and curves in the sky or directs his casts with the precision of a laser. They are simply fun to cast. You don't need to have a fly on the leader or even be near the water. There is pure enjoyment in putting these finely tuned, graceful instruments through their paces, like choreographing a dance. And the practice keeps your timing sharp. Several times a week, weather permitting, I find myself fly casting on the lawn just for the playfulness of it. I haven't yet achieved a take from a bird as author Tom McGuane did by casting a piece of red thread to a robin in his book *The Longest Silence,* but I'm working on it.

Most of the saltwater fly fishing that I do is geared to eight- or nine-weight rods, sometimes a ten. Rods heavier than that enter the realm of big game and are injurious to my shoulders and forearms if cast relentlessly. My current workhorse favorite started out as a nine-foot Loomis for a seven-weight line. With six inches broken off the tip, it now casts a ten-weight line like a

Keep the Faith oil on linen 11 x 16 inches 1992

cannon while weighing only three and a half ounces. Lighter rods raise eyebrows but will do the job nicely if small enough flies are used. A seven can handle most of the inshore game fish in New England waters if lifting power is not required, and even a six can fight a ten-pound bluefish to a standstill. I always thought that fives, however, were only for extremists like Howard Gaber, a Montauk veteran who found his way to the Vineyard in the early 1980s along with compatriots Ron Hall and Ken and Lori Vanderlaske.

They are all superb anglers. Ken's first bass at Squibnocket Point on the Vineyard's south shore weighed an even sixty pounds, and Lori went on to catch the women's world-record fly rod bluefish for twenty-pound tippet: eighteen pounds, eleven ounces. Ron and Howard were masters with surf rods and tremendously gifted freshwater fly fishermen with great depth of trout and Atlantic salmon experience.

When I invited Howard to join me for an evening of fly rodding for stripers at Lobsterville in July 1988, I was shocked when he showed up with a five-weight trout rod and a Hardy Princess reel. Not only did he make no apologies for his undergunned tackle, he told me with classic Gaber assurance that he would probably outfish me. I'd seen enough of his angling prowess not to bet against him. He is a cutting-edge and hugely competitive fisherman who always stretches the boundaries and manages to come out on top. A third member of our party was my friend Bob Stinson, an Australian with great angling talent and immense enthusiasm.

We ran smack into a classic blitz. From 9:30 p.m. until 2 the next morning, fishing the bottom of the falling tide and the start of the rise, we caught and released eighty-four fly rod stripers from seven to fifteen pounds. The bass were close, often right in the wash. If we got our feet wet, we were too far into the water. We could see their dim shadows in the pale moonlight and sight cast to them.

Afternoon in September oil on canvas 18 x 36 inches 1982

Top rod? Gaber with thirty-four stripers on that five-weight. And he beached his fish as quickly as Stinson and I did on our eights. A couple of nights later, just to prove it was no accident, he fished through the night and caught thirty-eight more. I thought it was interesting that he did it with a five-weight, but I was not tempted to go that light myself. It seemed too extreme and only for an angler of outrageous self-confidence and skill.

And then there was Roberto Germani, a mystical angler who was pulled relentlessly by the primitive forces of the sea. A gifted artist who spent nineteen years on a painting before deciding that it was finished. A fly tier who named his flies and gave me one called "Mary

Magdelene's Little Sister with Lipstick." A fisherman who temporarily gave up fly casting for handlining, using a heave-and-haul technique with a stripping basket and an old revolving spool reel strapped to his waist, laughing and whooping in huge glee as he played tug of war with stripers and blues. A man who pioneered the use of a kayak for fishing on the Vineyard. Who also pioneered his signature use of a grocery

Roberto Germani and the author in Cape Pogue Pond in 1986.

shopping basket for a stripping basket.

And, yes, a man who came to use a five-weight fly rod after years of subduing blues, bonito, false albacore, and stripers up to thirty-five pounds on sevens and eights. He had decided that those were big-game rods, and that he wanted a more sporting proposition, insisting that fish should be fought with the drag of the reel, not the power of the rod. No one could argue with the results. One morning in the autumn of 1990, fishing with his five-weight from the shore in the strong current of Cape Pogue Gut on Chappaquiddick, Roberto landed two huge albies that were estimated to weigh sixteen and eighteen pounds. Those fish would have been more than a challenge for any other angler using a ten-weight.

Then my son Everett, who likes living on the edge, was influenced by Roberto and got a relatively stiff five-weight of his own. One of his first catches was a thirty-six-inch, eighteen-pound striper, but shortly after that he broke the rod and could not replace it. His next five-weight was a

Behind Menemsha oil on linen 16 x 24 inches 2009

noodle that was not suitable for saltwater, and he gave it up. Roberto died too soon, and Howard Gaber moved on to salmon in Iceland and Russia and bought an offshore boat to chase tuna off Montauk.

Five-weight fly rods disappeared from my radar screen until the spring of 2001 when Dr. Jim Malm and I fished the worm hatch in Lake Tashmoo on the Vineyard's north shore. The stripers that feed on the emergent worms had been on the small side in recent years, and Jim had bought a five-weight Orvis trout rod weighing only three ounces and a light large arbor reel to get maximum fun from this fishery. I had been having shoulder problems and felt I needed a lighter fly rod to get me through the recovery process. I tried his and found that it was a joy to cast, had ample backbone, and was pain-free for my shoulder. I acquired one of my own.

Shortly thereafter, on a June night with a light southwest wind and fog, I tried it at Lobsterville. Shades of Howard Gaber, thirteen years later: from dusk until midnight I caught eighteen stripers from twenty-four to twenty-nine inches, roughly seven to twelve pounds. I could have stayed longer and caught more, but that seemed sufficient. I was no longer interested in running up the numbers. The rod was entirely adequate and great fun.

The following winter I took it to the Bahamas for bonefish. When I told them what I was going to do, Cooper Gilkes, iconic owner of Coop's Bait and Tackle in Edgartown, and Nelson Bryant, outdoor columnist for *The New York Times,* both said I was crazy and that it was not enough rod for the gray ghost of the flats. I wasn't worried, however. I knew how it had performed on stripers, and I was confident that it could handle the four- to eight-pound bonefish that I was likely to encounter. The very first day, wading in shin-deep water, I stalked a school of six tailing fish and was eventually able to make a good cast with a pink puff. One of them hit and was off to the races with a searing one-hundred-

The Gut on Chappaquiddick—a fly fishing mecca.

yard run followed by two more that got well into backing, and then some more dogged stuff until I could reach down and grasp him behind the gills, turn him over, and remove the hook. He measured twenty-seven inches—about seven and a half pounds—a very respectable bonefish on any fly rod, and a trophy on a five-weight. A "trip fish" in Bahamian vernacular—one that made the entire trip a success.

This is a terrific rod for bonefish wading, when you can maneuver to put the wind where you want it. And overloaded with a seven-weight line, it handles the wind very well anyway. I took several more bones from four to seven pounds on it, and never used the six-, seven-, and eight-weight rods that I had also brought on the trip. A magic wand, indeed, that five-weight, almost an extension of your arm and so light and well balanced that casting is effortless and graceful. I think I've joined the extremists. ◆

Permit

It was April 1976 or so, and Spider Andresen and I were stuck in traffic on Duval Street in Key West, opposite the Bull and Ale, where a comely waitress was serving beer at tables on the sidewalk to a group of bikers whose black steeds crowded the curb. As we were admiring her looks, she put down her tray, took the bottom of her shirt in both hands, raised it over her head, and did a shake-and-shimmy with her naked breasts as though this congested thoroughfare was a private club.

This was my introduction to the bawdy, anything-goes Key West that I had read about in Tom McGuane's *Ninety-Two in the Shade,* and which I would revisit several times for its great flats fishing and interesting lifestyle. Spider, who had been my cohort at *Salt Water Sportsman* magazine, had been to Key West before and had arranged a dual charter trip for us with our friends Gil Drake and his wife Linda, both of whom were highly regarded charter skippers.

The next afternoon Linda introduced me to a species of fish that would elude me for the next twenty or so years. We had been casting to barracuda and tarpon when she spied a sickle fin that put urgency in her whispered "Permit!"

Clouds over Yucatan oil on panel 8 x 12 inches 1998

She impaled a crab on a hook attached to six-pound-test monofilament on a light spinning rig and pointed to where she had seen the fin. I lobbed the crab to the spot and let it sink. The fish took and immediately launched a fast, powerful run off the flat, while Linda followed with the electric motor. The permit reached deep water, and fifty-five minutes later the line fatigued and broke. I had never seen the fish, which Linda thought weighed about twenty pounds. Only later did I learn that this species is considered the premier quarry for dedicated flats anglers and is notoriously fickle when it comes to taking a fly.

In the ensuing years on infrequent trips to the south I targeted fly rod tarpon at Key West for a while, then bonefish in the Bahamas and Belize, sometimes getting a random chance to cast at permit, but never hooking up. Once my son Everett and I saw a huge school of large permit at Deep Water Cay in the Bahamas. Our guide, David Pinder Sr., estimated that there were eighty fish up to forty pounds and said he had never before seen that many. They kept milling around a flat, giving us numerous casting opportunities, but they would pay no attention whatsoever to our flies. It seemed probable that they were frightened and harassed by predators, probably sharks, that we could not see.

At other times I had casts to a large permit following a ray at Andros, to tailers at Bimini and Belize, and to a departing school at Key West. On that occasion, my fly dropped behind the last fish in the school, which promptly did a U-turn and bit it without getting hooked. My guide, Gil Drake, said he had never seen a permit behave that way. As time went on, I became resigned to not catching one, even though I did a lot of reading on the subject and greatly envied those who had succeeded. The odds against hooking and landing a sighted permit on a fly seemed too long for a New Englander who made only one or two southern trips a year in the winter when this fishing is not at its peak.

Search for a sickle fin.

Then in 1998 I was invited by my friends Frank and Cynthia Browning to join a congenial group at Boca Paila Fishing Lodge on the Yucatan coast of Mexico. The time was mid-April, and the booking agent's brochure boasted that "grand slams" of bonefish, tarpon, and permit occurred regularly. *This,* I thought, *might be my chance to break the permit jinx.* The leader of the fishing group, Malcolm MacLean, knew about my quest and graciously assigned me to a guide who was a permit specialist, Victor Dcol, an intense Mayan whose features looked as though they had been lifted from the nearby ancient ruin at Tulum.

The lodge is located on a thin strip of barrier beach between the Caribbean and a vast system of lagoons and flats dotted with small uninhabited mangrove islands, all part of the 1.3-million-acre Sian Ka'an Biosphere Reserve.

It is a naturalist's paradise, abounding in marine and avian species. There are numerous channels or *bocas* ("mouths" in Spanish) that connect the lagoon to the open ocean, and it is through these inlets that permit and other species enter to feed on the flats.

That spring the winds howled throughout the southern latitudes, blowing out the fishing in many areas. The Yucatan did not escape, and I arrived to find storm-tossed seas, heavy cloud cover, and water that was so roiled and "thick" that sight fishing was difficult at best. There was a surreal atmosphere around the comfortable seaside lodge: army troops in half-tracks patrolled the beach at night, the cardinal of Mexico was staying next door, and gale winds blasted beach sand under the doors and through shuttered windows while we regaled each other with fish tales, warmed up with good booze and excellent food. One of the group, Philip Dresdner of Princeton, New Jersey, had once caught a sixty-pound Atlantic salmon on a fly in Canada, a feat so astonishing that the rest of us did little or no boasting about our own angling accomplishments.

The first morning Victor and I found small bonefish in a brackish estuary within five minutes of leaving the dock. I hooked one on my first cast, lost it, hooked another on my second cast, and landed it. Then I told Victor that I would not cast at any more bones, that it was permit or nothing. He looked at me steadily, asked if I meant the entire week, and then nodded. I had signed on for six days in an open sixteen-foot skiff with a stranger from a foreign culture on an improbable mission to catch a mysterious, neurotic creature that looked like a slice of the moon.

Here's how it went, according to the notes I took:

Day 1: Mostly spent waiting for clouds to disperse so that we could see any permit that came our way. Three or four did, their dark fins and sharp tails erratically cleaving the surface and making my pulse rate soar. They paid no attention to my flies. Victor and I get along well

The Messenger oil on panel 11 x 14 inches 1998

in spite of language limitations; both of us are intense about the quest.

Day 2: More clouds and wind. No permit spotted. Zero casts.

Day 3: Less wind, but the fish are still elusive. I cast at four, but no takers. Victor is getting tense. I am starting to enjoy the perversity of it all. That night I say prayers to Alachkai, the Mayan god of fish.

Day 4: More strong wind. Four casts to permit. One hit but dropped the fly. We quit early, and I jogged along the beach to ease the growing frustration. A Mayan trio played music at dinnertime, and, as was our group's custom on past trips, the men danced with owner/chef Polly Gonzales. Two small permit had been caught by other guests blind casting with crabs, and everyone but I had caught plenty of bonefish.

Day 5: Calmer, no clouds. More than a dozen casts. Three bumps, but no hookups. Saw a couple of very large permit that Victor estimated at thirty-five and fifty pounds.

Day 6: The last day. Sand had again piled into my room, carried by the night winds like a sandstorm in the Sahara. As I was standing on the beach watching the sun rise, a native dog walked by and sat down sphinxlike in front of me. Perhaps it was an omen sent by Alachkai. There were clouds, wind, and only one cast in the morning, but it became much sunnier and calmer after lunch. Victor and I headed north for a last attempt. We had become pals in this apparently hopeless endeavor. I let him cast my rod in the morning, and he said that "Kib" was a Mayan name.

By 3:30 p.m. I had made eight casts, all refused or unseen, and then Victor changed my leader from fifteen-pound-test to ten, and tied on one of his own flies that had snake skin glued onto its back. On what would have been virtually my last cast of the trip I had a long crosswind left-handed shot to four tailing permit. I stripped twice, let the fly drop to the bottom, and—eureka!—a take. Extremely powerful first

On the sixth day.

run, about 150 yards. Then Victor followed the fish with the boat, and I regained line. Three times I had the leader to the rod tip, and each time the permit ran out all of the fly line again. My heart was in my mouth as I wondered if the ten-pound tippet and the connecting knots would hold. Finally he rolled on his side and Victor netted this beautiful, otherworldly, powerful creature that had bewitched me for so long. He estimated it at fifteen pounds. A thirty-minute fight on a nine-weight. My feelings of elation and sense of mission accomplished were beyond words. We high-fived, photographed and released the catch, and toasted Alachkai with a beer. We had fished intensely for six days for that permit, and it was worth every minute.

Pondering the experience in retrospect, I feel I won't try to repeat it. And yet it was one of the consummate experiences of my angling life. Certainly I'll be evermore searching for that sickle fin every time I am flats fishing. Perhaps Alachkai will look favorably upon me again. ◆

Alou

I was fishing under a bridge in Islamorada, Florida, one night in the spring of 1966 and struck up a conversation with an angler who was from New York, and, like myself, a striped bass fisherman. He told me that he had been having great success on Long Island with a new lure called the Alou Eel. I had never heard of it, but when I got back to my office at *Salt Water Sportsman* magazine in Boston I did a bit of detective work, found the address of the Alou Tackle Company in Bayside, New York, and wrote asking if I could procure a couple of their lures to field test at Martha's Vineyard. In short order I received a package of Alou Bass Eels with a cover letter from company president Al Reinfelder telling me to enjoy them and let him know how they worked.

The Bass Eels weighed three ounces and consisted of metal swimming heads armed with 4/0 hooks attached to soft plastic imitation eels of various colors with a second hook at the tail end. The Alou Eel was designed by Al and his partner Lou Palma, hence the name Alou. As soon as I put one in the water and saw its swimming action, I knew bass would find it irresistible.

Into Twilight oil on linen 24 x 36 inches 1984

One night that July I was fishing on the Vineyard's South Beach with Bob Pond, manufacturer of the famed line of Atom plugs, and Dick Hathaway, renowned as one of the greatest surf striper fishermen on the entire East Coast. Both men were casting Atom swimmers, but I had decided to experiment and stick with Alou Eels. Fishing was slow, and the bass that were there were picky. By the time we quit, Pond and Hathaway had each caught one bass on Atoms. I had caught three on Alou Eels. The venerable Atom swimmer had been outfished by a new artificial. When I relayed the news to Al Reinfelder, I think I heard him cheer all the way from Long Island.

Later that autumn I began hooking big bass in the forty-pound class on Alou Eels cast from a small aluminum boat that I would carry over the breakwater at the parking lot at Squibnocket on the Vineyard's south shore and then launch through the surf and row or motor to the nearby striper grounds. I had been fishing this way for several years and had taken a good number of large fish up to forty-eight pounds on plugs, primarily Reverse Atoms, whose topwater antics provoked explosive surface hits from those big stripers. But I had lost more bass than I had caught. The problem was that many of the fish would entangle the plugs in the rocks and kelp and then simply straighten out the hooks and escape. The biggest of those bass was the largest striper I have ever seen. It hit a Reverse Atom right at the gunwale, and my friend Stuart Hunter and I both saw it clearly. It quickly scraped the plug out on a nearby rock and got away, and we looked at each other and simultaneously said, "Eighty pounds!" It looked *that* big.

I had caught a sixty-pounder at Cuttyhunk a few years earlier and had seen Ralph Grey's famed sixty-eight-pounder at Provincetown. This seemed a whole lot bigger. One of its scales remained impaled on a treble hook, and I sent it to the marine biological lab in Woods Hole to see if the fish's age could be determined; however,

Striper oil on linen 24 x 36 inches 1983

it turned out to be a regenerated scale from an old injury and could not provide the information I sought. In any case, I felt as though I'd had a hold of a world-record striper for a few moments.

Once I started using Alou Eels, the problem of losing fish was largely solved, because the bass could not readily tangle that lure in the rocks, and if they did, the strong single hook would not straighten out the way the trebles had. I took numerous stripers over forty pounds to a top of fifty-five-and-a-quarter on Bass Eels and their bigger Cow Killer cousins. I sent reports to Reinfelder about this fishing, and the following autumn he brought his family to the Vineyard to spend a weekend and see what I was doing. I got up early on the first morning while he was still sleeping and launched my one-man nine-foot tin boat at Squibnocket at first light and was back on the beach thirty minutes later with forty-five- and forty-three-pounders caught on amber Alou Eels. That did it. Al would spend a lot of time here in the future, and I never again got on the water before he did.

I had taken an immediate liking to Al. He was easygoing and intense at the same time, and very passionate about striped bass and life in general. We did some surf casting together, and he was clearly an excellent fisherman. I learned that he was also an environmental activist, a lecturer, a musician, an artist, and an author. He wrote a lovely poem about his final Sunday of that trip, and I felt I had only scratched the surface of an extraordinary man. I invited him and his partner Lou Palma to come back the following year, along with another friend who was also a lure manufacturer—Art Lavallee, president of Acme Tackle Company in Rhode Island. Al brought along his own tin boat, a twelve-foot Starcraft, and I had upgraded to a twelve-foot Aero-Craft; so the four of us, two in each boat, could launch at Squibnocket and fish the rocks with Alou Eels in the morning. We took big fish regularly, and then we fished the beaches in the afternoon and evening.

At night, joined by our friend Dan Bryant and with plenty of Scotch whiskey under our belts along with wonderful dinners cooked by Palma, Al and Lou taught us the secrets of bridge fishing, which they had honed to a fine art on Long Island where the practice was illegal and where they had to keep one step ahead of the cops. Al wrote an article about it for the *Long Island Fisherman* titled "Outlaws on the Bridge."

He had developed a jig called the Bait Tail

Al Rienfelder, Lou Palma, and Art Lavallee weigh a thirty-eight-pounder caught on an Alou Eel off Squibnocket from a tin boat in 1968.

that we cast from the up-tide side of Edgartown's Anthiers bridge into the tide and then let it bounce back toward us. Bass would hit when it reached the shadow line, and with very heavy tackle we would try to hold their heads above water so they could not swim under the bridge and cut us off. The thrashing sounds of those lassoed fish were like small cars falling into the water! It was exciting stuff and a grand way to end those very full days when four friends were whacking bass almost around the clock, always goading each other on with sharply barbed wit. And this was just the beginning. During the next few years, Al, Lou, Dan, and I fished together innumerable times, frequently joined by Nelson Bryant and Spider Andresen, and it was the best of times and we were the best of friends.

Within a couple of years Al had bought land on the Island and built a cabin for himself and his family, and there were wonderful evenings there and in my house listening to Al play his guitar and harmonica and sing his favorite songs surrounded by our families and friends. He had upgraded from a tin boat to a nineteen-foot Mako, and won the boat striper division of the Vineyard Derby in 1969. He and Lou became regulars on the fishing scene here. In 1971 the three of us, fishing together in the same boat, took first, second, and third place in the boat striper division of the Derby. My forty-seven-pounder was the winner in spite of Lou's stomping on it in a failed effort to make it regurgitate the contents of its stomach and thereby weigh less than his own big bass.

After asking forgiveness from God for what he was about to do, Al had introduced us to live-lining bunker or menhaden for striped bass. It was an absolutely deadly method that had not been used here before, and we swept the Derby using bunker that we traveled all the way to New Bedford to snag. My winning fish, however, was taken on a jointed Creek Chub Giant Pikie with an eelskin stretched over it. Al and Lou were using live bunker that had raised a school of big

Along the North Shore oil on linen 24 x 36 inches 1985

stripers, including mine, and gotten them into something approaching a feeding frenzy. I was trying to be a purist with an artificial lure, but convinced no one, myself included, that the bass would have acted so aggressively had it not been for those frantic, live-lined bunker in the water.

Al had become a luminary. In addition to designing lures for the Garcia Corporation, which had bought out the original Alou Tackle Company, he was a profuse writer and a champion of several causes that sought to preserve our natural environment. He was investigating, writing, and lecturing about ecology as well as fishing, and he brought to everything he did a charisma and a contagious enthusiasm that attracted people to his causes.

He became president of the Striped Bass Fund, which sought to protect the future of the species. He seemed bigger than life: a wonderful father, husband, and friend, a superb fisherman, a philosopher, a writer, and a performer of music that I could listen to all night long. His energy and life force seemed boundless. And then in an instant he was gone, killed at age thirty-six in a canoeing accident on his beloved Delaware River on May 18, 1973. A bright and shining light had been extinguished and with it the joy and meaning he had brought to so many lives. His friends were devastated. Lou Palma quit fishing for more than fourteen years. I resigned from *Salt Water Sportsman* a couple of months later to pursue a career as an artist. I probably would have done so anyway, but I often wonder if his death had not been a strong factor in my decision. With Al gone, the fishing world was never the same.

Happily, however, Lou returned to the Vineyard and to fishing in the late 1980s, and we were gradually able to reestablish strong vestiges of the old days. And we sometimes still cast an Alou Eel, even though that lure has long been out of production and is now a collector's item. ◆

Originally published in Martha's Vineyard Magazine *(September/October 2005).*

Metaphor oil on linen 24 x 36 inches 2008

New Millennium

January 1, 2000. A clear, calm start to the new millennium. Temperature in the mid-twenties. A white frost on the ground. I went to my camp at Deep Bottom Cove on Tisbury Great Pond, where the tableau was stunning. Skim ice covered most of the cove, but there was a patch of open water by the dock where two swans rested atop perfect reflections. Further to the south another pool of water held six mallards that noisily departed upon my arrival, while on the ice itself an otter lay sphinxlike with raised head. The ice was talking excitedly about the dawn of the millennium—creaks, whispers, grunts—incessant chatter as the heat of a new day and a light southerly breeze nudged it awake.

My thoughts turned to the big school of striped bass that had been locked in the pond when its temporary opening to the Atlantic Ocean had been closed by winds and tides in the late summer. There have always been stripers that winter-over in this pond, and through the years there have been tales of large hauls of bass that have been seined here, either illegally or as by-catch in nets set for herring or white perch. But this year was different: more bass than usual had entered the pond and had simply stayed,

The Cove oil on linen 30 x 44 inches 1982

probably because there was so much to eat. There were huge numbers of juvenile alewives that had been spawned in the spring at the confluence of fresh and saltwater, as well as baby menhaden that had come in through the inlet when it was bulldozed open in late summer. I guessed the bass numbered a thousand or so; my friend Nelson Bryant believed there were at least three thousand. My New Year's resolution was to prospect these waters as soon as the weather allowed, find where the fish wintered, and try to catch some.

Soon thereafter there were three weeks of serious cold, single-digit temperatures that sealed all the Island ponds under six to ten inches of black ice and produced the best skating and ice boating that anyone had seen in many years. You could walk, skate, or sail all the way from the parking lot at Squibnocket to the outer beach, while Harlock's Pond at Seven Gates Farm was a perfect mirror on which our family and friends skated every day. Nothing thawed until early February,

and I wondered if the imprisoned stripers and whatever baitfish they fed on had survived.

March 6 was the day to find out, with calm winds, a bright sun, and the temperature in the fifties. I launched my fourteen-foot *Tin Boat* and prospected a number of the spots where the bass had been most numerous the previous autumn, using a baitcasting outfit armed with a Joppa Jig, a leadhead with a soft plastic swimming tail that could be fished at various depths, including bouncing it off the bottom. I was encouraged not to find any signs of winterkilled bass or their prey, but after a couple of hours I still hadn't had a hit and had decided that the fish were too dormant. Giving it a last try in another spot, I thought I felt a familiar tap, and on the next cast I was solidly hooked up to a striper that fought with all the strength and energy that I would expect in the spring or autumn. The fish I brought to boat was in beautiful shape—bright and silvery, fat and sassy at twenty-two inches. After releasing him I had several more hits

Night Coming On oil on linen 10 x 16 inches 2003

and landed another of sixteen inches. Mission accomplished. I had pioneered a brand-new winter sportfishery. Later in March, by then technically springtime, I found the stripers again and landed ten of them up to twenty-four inches in length. I kept all of this a delicious secret and felt that the New Millennium had gotten off to a wonderful start. ◆

Originally published in Martha's Vineyard Magazine. *(Not Summer 2004–2005 issue).*

Tarpon

Fly rodding for big tarpon on the flats is arguably the most exciting form of angling that man has dreamed up. The sight of a hundred-pounder swimming into casting range can cause knees to shake, hands to tremble, and the best-laid game plans to evaporate, while the prospect of actually trying to tame a six-foot acrobatic monster on a mere fly rod is enough to make strong men hesitate.

I had seen a few of the domesticated resident tarpon of Key West harbor when I began fishing there in the mid-1970s, but it wasn't until quite a bit later that I found the time and resolve to fish for their mysterious migratory cousins who appear each spring, traveling north from uncharted waters in the ocean depths and from Central America. In May 1984 I booked several days of tarpon charters with Linda and Gil Drake, knowing that—with such excellent guides—I would have a good chance of at least getting a cast at one.

The first morning's trip was with Linda, and we boarded her sixteen-foot skiff at first light on a calm morning to make the nineteen-mile trip west to the Marquesas. At the time, Linda was the only woman in the Keys who was a professional

The Bahamas oil on linen 14 x 21 inches 1985

flats-fishing guide. She was a master of her trade and a superb angler in her own right, as well as being drop-dead attractive. The fact that I would probably make a fool of myself in front of her added an edge to my already considerable nervousness about testing my angling prowess on the silver king. I had been reading, hearing, and thinking about tarpon for years, but had never made a cast at one. I had zero expectations of success, and only hoped that I would not screw up too badly when the time came.

The sun was still low in the sky when Linda eased up on the throttle and began poling us across a lovely, windless Marquesas flat as I got ready on the casting deck. Getting ready means stripping about seventy feet of line onto the deck, casting it, and then retrieving and piling it in neat coils so that it won't foul when cast at your quarry. Then, with a few feet of line hanging from the rod tip, the rod in your casting hand and the fly held between the thumb and forefinger of the other hand, you assume a posture that will allow you to make a quick, accurate cast to the spot where the fly will intercept the fish's path of travel.

A myriad of things can go wrong and often do, from impaling the guide on the backcast to stepping on the line as it flies off the deck. The readiness stance itself can become exhausting after a while. On this morning, however, I had been on deck for only a few minutes when Linda stage-whispered "Tarpon at ten o'clock, one hundred feet!" Sure enough, there it was: a large gray shadow coming straight at us. There wasn't any time to become nerve-frayed. I made a couple of backcasts and sent the fly toward the fast-closing fish. It was on target. "Strip!" Linda said. I did, once, twice, three times, and then came tight on the take. I struck two or three times to set the hook and then watched in utter astonishment as the water erupted and a huge silver creature climbed in contorted curves toward the sky, shaking droplets of water everywhere, and then dropped back with a thunderous crash, only to swim toward us and repeat the gymnastics but this time closer so it seemed as though we were looking straight up at him. I wondered what would happen if he came down in the boat.

When he fell we were sprayed by the impact, then he greyhounded a couple of hundred feet and jumped again and then again. We were in five or six feet of water, and Linda kept the boat between him and deep water, where he could have sounded. As a result he jumped time after time trying to throw the hook, and after nearly an hour he was exhausted by the pressure of the rod and his own acrobatics. I brought him to the gunwale where Linda grabbed the leader, removed the hook, and helped him regain his equilibrium before releasing him. Then she called her husband on the radio and said, "Gil, Kib just caught a 125-pound tarpon!"

Talk about beginners' luck. On my first tarpon day, on my first cast, I had caught a 125-pound trophy that exceeded my wildest expectations in every respect. As the adrenaline

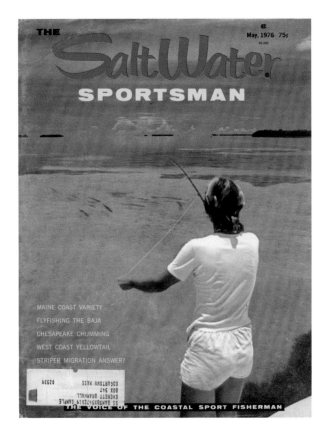

Linda Drake casts to a school of big tarpon on the cover of the May 1976 Salt Water Sportsman. *Photograph by Gil Drake.*

waned, my knees shook at the picture of that rattling silver monster airborne almost directly over the boat, and to this day it remains my most heart-stopping angling memory.

Naturally that fish was the pinnacle of my tarpon experience. I hooked—"jumped"—seven others with both Linda and Gil during the ensuing days, but failed to bring any to the boat, losing them to thrown hooks, parted lines, and any number of the angler errors that I had miraculously avoided with that first fish.

On another day I also came close to losing my life. Linda and I had gone to the Marquesas with the wind building, and by the time we headed home to Key West it was blowing a good twenty knots. We were running directly into it when we crossed Boca Grande channel, and the seas had gotten big. This was dangerous water for a sixteen-foot flats skiff, and no other boats were around. I was sitting in the stern next to Linda when we came off the top of a wave, a gust caught the airborne bow of the boat, and we were blown absolutely vertical. We hung there for an eternity, straight up and down, wondering whether we would go over backward and sink. Linda wondered what kind of shark would eat her, and I realized that my family would never know what had happened to me. Finally the skiff fell forward, not backward, and we lived. It was as close a call as I've ever had on the water. We redistributed weight by having me sit forward and pounded safely home, but Linda was so shaken that she cancelled the next couple of days' trips.

I returned to Key West in April the following year for another crack at tarpon and managed to boat a 50-pounder with Gil and jump half a dozen others, including another estimated 125-pounder that broke off with a resounding snap when I stepped on the fly line as it was uncoiling from the deck. All I could do was laugh.

By the end of that trip my interest in tarpon had waned. I found it exhausting to spend entire days tensed in the bow searching for hints of fish and sometimes never making a cast in eight hours on the water. And I came to the realization that I was a wrist fisherman, not a back fisherman; I preferred fly rodding for more manageable species on lighter tackle.

Tarpon were simply too damn big as far as I was concerned, much more a big-game quarry than one suitable for fly tackle. The twelve-weight fly rods that are used for this kind of fishing are truly heavy artillery and are neither pleasing nor graceful to cast. They certainly do not fit any definition of light tackle, but their heft and lifting power are needed to subdue their outsize quarry in a reasonable amount of time. I had been using my own outfit—a ten-weight Fenwick Boron-X rod that had tremendous backbone—and it proved adequate to the task. Even that rod was too stiff and heavy for my tastes, however, and I finally sold it. For me one of the joys of fly fishing is the delicacy and grace of the tackle, and the heavy stuff gives me no pleasure.

Fifteen years later, in April 2000, I needed a tarpon fix again and went to Marathon in the Keys for a weekend of fishing with guide David Kreshpane. I jumped a forty-pound tarpon on an eight-weight. That, I felt, was about right. A big enough fish on a rod light enough to be fun to handle. Who could ask for anything more? ◆

The Derby

The Martha's Vineyard Striped Bass Derby was created in 1946 in an attempt to extend the Island's tourist season by promoting its excellent autumn fishing, and it caught on in a big way. In its first year, one thousand anglers from twenty-nine states came to compete for prizes and glory. Once it began, the Derby assumed a momentum of its own that has propelled it through the years, through changes in management, even through the mid-1980s' collapse of the striped bass stocks. Today it has become a venerable institution that draws around three thousand participants each year from mid-September to mid-October.

The original emphasis on striped bass has broadened to include bluefish, bonito, and false albacore, with separate categories for shore fishermen, boat fishermen, and fly rodders, as well as juniors, who are indoctrinated at an early age into the contest's prestige-ridden aura. The Derby is now run by a dedicated volunteer committee of fishermen who give their time year-round to its planning and implementation. Many participants are Derby veterans who show up year after year, lending a wonderful air of camaraderie and continuity to the competition.

Hookup at Dawn oil on linen 20 x 20 inches 1985

One of them, Jerry Jansen from New York City, joined every year from 1947 to 2007. There are Derby friendships and rivalries that span decades. Some anglers abandon wives, girlfriends, sleep, and jobs during the entire contest. Derby committee member Cooper Gilkes likens it to astronaut training. The Derby is marked by intense and warmhearted competition and by the feeling of a grand, high-spirited party that permeates every segment of life on the Island while celebrating the golden days of autumn and the attendant migrations of game fish along its coastline.

As a boy who was brought up in a family fishing contest on the Jersey coast, I couldn't wait to try my hand in the Derby, which began the year after I first set foot on the Island. However, I was a summer kid and had to leave just before it started, so it wasn't until 1951 when I was in college with my own car that I was able to return to the Vineyard in the autumn and compete in it. While my Princeton classmates cheered and partied at football weekends, I

fished the south shore and Chappaquiddick from a 1936 Ford coupe whose oversize tires, backed by a shovel and tow rope, enabled it to function reasonably well as a beach buggy.

My Derby performance was humbling. I could catch my share of bass and blues, but nothing big enough to win anything but an occasional daily prize. My heroes were the all-night hardcore experts like Bud Oliver who weighed in the forty-pounders, but I could not figure out where they fished or how. In 1955 I graduated from college with six months to kill before going into the U.S. Army to fulfill my R.O.T.C. obligation, and went to work in my father's Wall Street municipal bond firm as the heir apparent. I quit after six weeks of utter boredom and went to the Vineyard to spend the rest of the summer commercial bluefishing with my friend Stuart Hunter, and then had the unparalleled luxury of being able to fish every single day and night of the Derby. First prize that year was awesome: a prefab camp on a building lot in Gay Head. I fished as hard as I knew how,

Shining Tide oil on linen 14 x 21 inches 1985

but didn't come close. The winner was Louise de Somov, wife of Sergei, the famed Mad Russian. Her forty-five-pound, nine-ounce bass was caught at Zacks Cliffs on an eel after the high

The author fishing at Stonewall Beach in 1956.
Photograph by Tess Bramhall.

tide and a flat tire had stranded their Jeep in its hiding place behind a rocky outcropping.

From then on I competed in the Derby every year except for 1983 and 1984, when I took an activist role in a boycott of the contest in an effort to have stripers eliminated from the prize structure. At that time striped bass stocks had declined to such an alarming extent that the species appeared in danger of extinction, and it seemed amoral to put a Derby bounty on their heads. The Derby Committee finally dropped stripers from the tournament in 1985, bowing to conscience and pressure from fishermen, sponsors, and the press, and did not reinstate them until 1994 when the species was officially declared restored. The restoration effort had included an Emergency Striped Bass Bill passed by the U.S. Congress and spearheaded by Massachusetts congressman Gerry Studds, and cooperative conservation legislation implemented by all the Atlantic coastal states from Maryland to Maine.

The vast majority of anglers enthusiastically

Wind from the Northeast oil on linen 30 x 40 inches 1985

supported and helped enforce the conservation efforts. Without stripers in the prize structure, the Derby lost some of its glamour but none of its popularity: numbers of entrants continued

The author's nine-foot tin boat with a forty-one-pound bass in the bow in 1961. He won the boat striper division of the Derby from this craft in 1967 with a forty-five-pounder.

to grow during the nine years that bass were absent, with bluefish, bonito, and false albacore taking up the slack.

I eventually caught some winners in the contest, with first-place boat stripers in 1967 and 1971, a winning bonito and winning fly rod striper in 1981, and fly rod–winning bonito in 1988, 1989, and 1992. The striper and two of the bonito were not only Derby winners, they also set new International Game Fish Association fly rod tippet world records.

The fly rod striper was the most memorable catch of my angling life.

It was October 16 on the downside of the full moon, near the end of the 1981 Derby. I had gone to Chappaquiddick late in the previous afternoon to fish with my friend and mentor Bruce Pratt. A decorated Vietnam veteran and the police chief of Edgartown, he had inspired me to get serious about fly rodding with his astonishing and consistent catches of large stripers up to thirty-eight pounds. He had generously taken me under his wing and in his understated and modest way had tutored me in every aspect of his angling art. That evening we fished an unproductive dusk tide together between the lighthouse and the windmill, and then Bruce told me that he wasn't feeling well and was going home. But he counseled me to stay because he had hooked a large bass there the previous night and lost it when he was spooled after an hour's fight. He gave me a few of his yellow deceivers, advising that the night was too bright for the white he usually favored. So I stayed.

About 11 p.m. the wind turned northeast, making casting difficult for the right-handers still on the beach. They all left. I have the good fortune to be able to cast with either arm; so I switched to lefty and hung on, taking a couple of catnaps in my Land Cruiser between casts. About 5 a.m. I was casting into the opaque false dawn when I had a solid take thirty feet out. I knew instantly that I was into the biggest fish I had ever hooked on a fly rod. I was using an eight-weight Daiwa and an inexpensive Abu reel that held 150 yards of backing, most of which disappeared on the first run.

I quickly decided on radical tactics to try to avoid being spooled like Bruce had. He had let his fish rest after each run. I didn't. When the first run ended I palmed the spool, kept a deep bend in the rod, and took a few steps backward until I could feel the striper's head turn toward me. Then I pumped and regained line until the second run, after which I repeated the process. And so on after the third. I never gave him a chance to regain his strength. Earlier in the season, salmon fishing in Iceland, I had pulled this rod against a scale and found that its maximum applied pressure was less than five pounds; therefore, I reasoned, the twelve-pound tippet could withstand the pressure of my walking backward up the beach against a heavy fish as long as I kept a bend in the rod and gave line if the bass lunged. It was a brawl! I kept turning his head and regaining line. Twenty minutes later I beached a forty-two-pound, fourteen-ounce striper and let out a whoop that could have been heard way over in Oak Bluffs. The IGFA awarded me the twelve-pound tippet world record for the catch, and it won the fly rod division of the Derby.

I have long felt something of a love-hate relationship for the Derby. I basically love fishing for its Zen qualities, for the intimate association it lets me make with the watery world which I love. I can happily spend an entire day on the water without catching anything particularly notable, perhaps simply observing and learning patterns of fish behavior and appreciating the attendant bird life, landscape, fauna, and cloud patterns. But when competition enters the picture, everything changes, including me. The school stripers that were so much fun become a disappointment when measured against the thirty-pounders that Danny Bryant and my brother, David, caught the same afternoon. The half dozen or so bonefish that my son Everett and I released in a fine day at the Andros Island Bonefish Tournament became bitter gruel when we learned that Jaime Boyle and Pip Winslow had boated twenty.

A wonderful day of fishing is ruined if a competitor does better. Although the fires of competition have cooled, those boyhood years of indoctrination into the family fishing contest left me with a competitive urge that I cannot seem to shed completely. My friend Nelson Bryant believes that competition has no place in fishing, and he has never entered the Derby. The late and singular Roberto Germani quit fishing the Derby because he could no longer bring himself to kill a fish in order to weigh it in. I agree in spirit, but I cannot help myself. I was imprinted at an early age.

And that competitive urge has been responsible for memorable catches that I would not have made otherwise. Like that big fly rod striper. Had it not happened during the Derby, I would never have fished through the night for twelve hours without so much as a hit until it came my way. So I dislike the Derby because it makes me push

Road to Cape Pogue oil on linen 13 x 21 inches 1982

myself beyond the level of pure contemplative enjoyment that I otherwise take from fishing. And because it has made others push themselves to extremes of misjudgment that, in a few cases, have resulted in disgrace and disqualification because of cheating, or, in other cases, fatal boating accidents. I also dislike the fact that it causes overcrowding at many of my favorite fishing sites. Yet I love the Derby because of its history and traditions, because of all the wonderful fishermen I have met, and, yes, because of the competition. It makes me fish harder and better in spite of myself. When I was elected to the newly created Derby Hall of Fame in 1999, I was deeply moved, though a bit apprehensive at the fact that I was the oldest living inductee. ◆

This is an amended version of an article published in Martha's Vineyard Magazine *(September/October 2003).*

Torpedoes on a Tippet

In 1955 a new species appeared in my fishing log with this entry: "Bonito driving us crazy—caught only one although they are thicker than fleas." This was prophetic. Bonito have been playing games with my mind ever since, and I have a love-hate relationship with them.

It is easy to love Atlantic bonito; they are beautiful, sleek game fish that will hit artificials, fight like demons, and are delicious to eat. It is also easy to hate them. They can be so finicky that it is masochistic to try to catch them. I have seen experienced anglers make a hundred or more casts into breaking bonito without getting a hit, and that sort of thing is either humiliating or funny, depending on your viewpoint. I've always felt that it is a mistake to take yourself too seriously when fishing for them.

July 27, 1981, was the day that made me a bonito addict. I had recently returned to the Vineyard from the Leirasveit River in Iceland, where I caught five Atlantic salmon weighing from six to thirteen pounds in a week of intense ten-hour angling days during which I had made at least a thousand blind casts. Now, back on the Vineyard on that July day, I launched my fourteen-foot tin boat at midday and ran smack into the season's first wave of incoming bonito off Menemsha. Schools were popping up

Sunrise at the Gut oil on panel 11 x 14 inches 1998

everywhere, and the fish were big and hungry. Furthermore, I had them to myself. This was an unexpectedly early arrival, and no one else was fishing for them.

Using the same eight-weight fly rod that I

Bob Stinson and Atlantic bonito.

had taken to Iceland, I sight-cast to breaking fish for the entire afternoon and hooked up twelve times. Every one of those bonito fought harder and took more line than the salmon. And it was much more exciting to cast to the furious surface explosions of the bonito than it had been to blind-cast hour after hour into water that may or may not have concealed a salmon who would not have been feeding anyway because he was there for sex, not food. And these bonito were right in my backyard. I was hooked.

Little scientific research has been done on bonito or their cousins, false albacore or "Little Tunny" or just plain albies. They are inhabitants of the open ocean, members of the mackerel family, and tunalike in appearance, speed, and stamina. Pound for pound, they are arguably the cream of the crop for inshore fly rodders in the Northeast. Their numbers in any given season are unpredictable and seem to be cyclical, but no one knows what governs the cycles beyond the fact that unusually cold water temperatures are a harbinger of lesser numbers. For some reason the numbers of Atlantic bonito seem to be decreasing as the years pass. Perhaps they are in a down cycle, or perhaps fishing pressure and competition from false albacore has simply made them harder to catch. Certainly my own intensity has diminished, and intensity has always been a key ingredient for fly rodding success with both bonito and albies.

Great anglers such as the late Roberto Germani could spend eight hours in a kayak waiting for a cast at them, and then go to bed and dream about these fish until he woke and began again, and he would live like that day after day, week after week, using five- to six-weight rods and tiny flies tied on #8 barbless hooks to take albies up to eighteen pounds.

If you don't have vast reserves of patience and intensity, it helps to be lucky. On October 3, 1989, I launched my tin boat in Edgartown at first light on a lovely calm morning and motored out around Cape Pogue and down East Beach where bonito had been showing regularly for the previous week or so. A little after 7 a.m. I found what I was looking for: a pod of big fish crashing into bait and no other boats nearby to spook them. I cut the motor, drifted into position with the tide, set my anchor, and waited for the fish to come to me. Before long, several were working the surface just where I hoped they would be, about sixty feet away.

After a couple of backcasts I was about to shoot the fly to them when a terrific fracas broke out right behind me. That's when I got lucky. I dropped the backcast, and the fly fell right into the mouth of a monster. That bonito peeled off more than 150 yards of backing, and I had to release the anchor and drift with him to avoid being spooled. Everything held together, and I eventually boated a 10.58-pounder to win the Derby and set a new world record for eight-pound-test tippet. With a fish caught on a dropped backcast! That says a lot about bonito fishing. Patience and intensity are huge, but nothing trumps luck.

False albacore—the bigger, tougher cousins of bonito—don't figure prominently in my fishing log for the simple reason that I don't catch many.

It's not that I don't try: they are terrifically exciting, but I seldom get in the albie groove. It must have something to do with chemistry.

I have had some good days, however—one of which was in late September 1990 when I boated ten from my boat off Chappaquiddick. I was emboldened enough by my success to invite *New York Times* outdoor columnist Nelson Bryant to accompany me the next day because I was so sure I would be able to stage a repeat performance. That's always a mistake. The fish were still there, but were acting differently, and for two hours we didn't get a hit. The wind kept building until it was a steady twenty, with thirty in gusts. Then I made a horrendous mistake by trying to change the direction of a cast in midair, and the windblown fly plucked Nelson's beret—with his World War II paratrooper's wings with two stars standing for his combat drops into Normandy and Holland—from his head and deposited it into the swift current. That was the low point of my angling life, but luckily the hat floated and we retrieved it without further ado.

At that point things could only get better, and they did, with each of us landing a couple of decent albies. They were the first Little Tunny that Nelson had caught, and when he wrote about the trip in his column a couple of days

Nelson Bryant's first Little Tunny.

later he commented that he could have boated a sixteen-pound bluefish in half the time that it took to land an eight-pound albie, and that this fish's "speed and dogged refusal to quickly come to net in the closing minutes of the game was startling."

As for its edibility, Nelson wrote, "Although I had been told that false albacore wasn't fit table fare, I couldn't believe there wasn't some way to make such a handsome fish palatable. That night I broiled, baked and poached albacore fillets and even marinated some thin slices of the fish in lemon juice for a kind of sashimi. The results were appalling to all save Norton the cat who will be eating false albacore for the next three weeks."

The third member of this family that I have targeted with fly rods is bluefin tuna when the youngsters—"footballs"—come close enough to the Vineyard. They are bigger, stronger versions of their bonito and albacore cousins and are wonderful fly rod challengers up to about thirty pounds or so. Heavier than that and I want nothing to do with them.

Everett Bramhall fly fishing for tuna from Shearwater *at the 31 Hole. Andrew Moore is hooked up on spinning, and Alley Moore will be soon.*

When Cooper Gilkes phoned to invite me to accompany him on a tuna fly rodding expedition aboard Captain Ross Roberts's *The Big Eye* in the summer of 1990, I accepted immediately. Coop was more excited than I'd ever heard him. He'd gone out with Roberts the prior day with a dozen tuna flies and lost all of them to rampaging bluefins while losing an entire fly line and burning out the drag on an expensive reel,

Everett Bramhall with a fly rod bluefin.

but still managed to boat a few small footballs.

We were aboard *The Big Eye* heading out of Edgartown Harbor by 7 a.m. the following Wednesday under perfect conditions: clear skies and no wind. The massive schools of bluefins that Ross had been finding sixty miles offshore had dispersed as the waters warmed to seventy-seven degrees, and the challenge was to find them again. He chose to prospect an area called the Star, twenty-five miles southeast of the Vineyard, because the water temperature there ranged from sixty-five to seventy-one degrees. Ross and mate Mickey Brand set out five trolling outfits on the starboard side and amidships on the stern, leaving the port side clear for a right-handed fly cast. As the name implies, school tuna usually travel together in large numbers. The game plan was to hook one on a trolling outfit, throw the boat out of gear, and then fly cast to the numerous fish that would be milling around their hooked companion. At 10:15 a school of tuna appeared in our wake, and two were hooked on the trolling outfits. This was my moment. I made my backcast, but the line wrapped around the bow rail, and by the time I cleared it the school had sounded. Classic snafu!

Later more bluefins showed in the wake, and I managed to get a fly to them, hooking and landing fifteen- and twenty-nine-pounders. The latter took thirty-five punishing minutes to land on my eight-weight, and that was enough to satisfy my fly rod tuna appetite for the next several years.

Then in August 2004 I chartered Captain Jaime Boyle for a trip to the 31 Hole south of the Vineyard where small bluefins were feeding in miles-long chum slicks created by groundfish discards from trawlers. Jaime picked up piles of the floating dead fish and created his own chum slick, which was quickly teeming with footballs, and my son-in-law Paul Schneider and I hooked up time and again on flies. I boated six fly rod bluefins on six consecutive casts and was simply too exhausted to make a seventh cast. After that I threw hookless popping plugs into the fish just for the excitement of seeing the explosive surface strikes.

On that day I became so seriously tuna-addicted that I purchased a twenty-three-foot SeaCraft so that I could pursue them on my own. However, conditions changed the next year, and small bluefins became increasingly scarce. I sold my tuna boat and went back to inshore fishing. ◆

Paul Schneider battling a bluefin on a heavy fly rod.

Shadow Fish

My son Everett and I were wading a small flat in the Bahamas hunting bonefish on a hot and windless day. We had taken a couple of fish earlier, but now nothing was moving in the sultry afternoon glare, and I was starting to lose the adrenaline edge that I usually carry with me on the flats. On the far side of the bay a single large mangrove bush began to shake and rustle as though possessed by a poltergeist of some sort, and then was still. A minute or so later it began moving again, audibly this time, and from it emerged a waterspout about ten feet high that circled in front of the mangrove while growing taller. When it reached a height of twenty feet or so, it started traveling erratically across the flat in our direction, speeding up as it came. We were about a hundred feet apart and could no longer hear each other because of the waterspout's noise.

We took off our hats and held tight to our tackle as this thing bore down and then went between us, clouding out the sun and buffeting us with spray and fifty-mile-per-hour winds. It traveled another quarter mile or so and then vanished, and it was as though nothing had ever happened. Everett and I talked about it in shaken

Clouds over Eleuthera oil on linen 12 x 16 inches 1999

wonderment for a while and then went back to fishing. Shortly he caught a twenty-nine-inch bonefish, the biggest either of us had ever taken on that flat. Had the waterspout been some sort of bonefish deity that vectored the big fish to him? Nothing would surprise me when it comes to the mysterious gray ghost of the flats.

While bonefish can indeed look gray under certain conditions, the nickname "gray ghost" is not an accurate color description. Its sides are silver mirrors that reflect its luminous surroundings, making it nearly invisible, while the back is a green-blue-gray pattern that blends perfectly with a typical grass flat. The fish is indeed ghostlike, however. Its ability to move through water only inches deep without disturbing the surface defies belief, and its camouflage is so effective that a shadow is often the only clue to its presence.

At times bonefish seem to emerge from thought to mirage to reality as though you have conjured them up from your imagination. On the other hand, the oversized and powerful gray tails are a giveaway when they are above the surface when rooting for crustaceans in shallow water, particularly late or early in the day when low, slanting sunlight illuminates them like flickering diamonds. Once I saw them silhouetted in the light beam of a just-risen full moon at Long Island in the Bahamas, a scene that will always remain indelibly etched in my mind.

Hunting bonefish is a challenge that offers rich aesthetic rewards as one explores a watery, ever-changing wilderness set off by saturated tropical colors. It is not relaxing. It demands intense concentration and experience to look through the water with Polaroid glasses rather than simply at it. To look for movement, shadows, or that slight change in shape that could be caused by your quarry. It is done while wading, seldom more than knee-deep, or from a boat poled across the air-thin water by a guide whose ability to spot fish is almost always better than yours. Sometimes, following his instructions

Shadowfish oil on paper 6 x 10 inches 2011

regarding distance and direction, you will cast to and hook bonefish that you never see. I feel that the overall experience is significantly diminished when this happens. The act of discovery—spotting the bonefish yourself—is one of the great joys and hurdles of the sport, and when the guide does it for you, something is lost. On the other hand, when you beat the guide to the spot, it is a moment of great satisfaction.

Flats are a world unto themselves, some of them glistening white sand; others grass, mud, or coral; some bone dry at low tide, and others always wearing a sheen of water. Some are attached to the mainland, others are far at sea where you wade like the first human to emerge from the ocean. Their shimmering beauty masks the fundamental truth that they are feeding grounds for predators, places of life and death and survival. They are dynamic, ever-changing zones of refracted light that are peaceful at times, violent at others, where bonefish come like phantoms from the deep to feed on crustaceans, worms, crabs, and shrimp, and where they themselves are sometimes the prey of sharks and barracuda. Finding these illusory fish brings observation to a high art and could be an end in itself, this first of a three-part sport.

Once you have spotted your quarry, the next challenge is to make a perfect cast. Not too close, because the fish will spook; not too far away, or he won't see the fly. There is no room for error. If it is done correctly and the retrieve is convincing and the fish isn't unnerved, the third part is astonishing. Bonefish are among the fastest, most powerful of any game fish, and when hooked will blast through the shallow water throwing spray and sand and bottom detritus in an unstoppable, primal surge to reach deep water. In all of the fishing I have done, the first run of a bonefish is consistently the most exciting. In addition to the pyrotechnics, there is the ripping sound of the line cutting through the shallow water as though the flat itself is being torn asunder.

Late Afternoon, Eleuthera oil on linen 14 x 21 inches 1986

The first time I experienced it was at the Deep Water Cay Club at the east end of Grand Bahama. I was wading in a mangrove-studded creek with a guide who spotted the fish. I made a decent cast, hooked up, and watched in open-mouthed amazement as the bonefish exploded across the flat and tore a circle around a dead bush. The line came tight. The tippet broke. The fish escaped. The bush fell into the water with a loud splash. I doubled over in laughter at the sheer mayhem of the encounter. In that moment I was hooked for life. Bonefish became and have remained my favorite fly rod quarry.

They are found in tropical waters world-wide, and I have hunted them throughout the Bahamas, the Florida Keys, the Yucatan, Belize, and Bermuda. I have never felt the urge to travel farther, say, to Christmas Island in the South Pacific, the Seychelles in the Indian Ocean, or Los Roques in Venezuela, all of which offer superb fishing. Why go so far when I can have an early breakfast in Boston and wade a bonefish flat in the Bahamas later the same day? I have seen and cast to truly large specimens at Islamorada, Bimini, and Andros, but never connected. Most of my fish have been between four and eight pounds, and each and every one of those provided a measure of excitement far out of proportion to its size. My biggest was an estimated ten-pounder.

On the day I caught that one, I had waded a Bahamian flat by myself for a couple of hours of a midday incoming tide and had tangled with enough medium-size bonefish to be content and ready to go home. Exiting the flat, I walked along the adjoining beach in the direction of my parked car. The onshore wind had increased in velocity, and now there were small waves breaking on the beach, and the flat was covered with whitecaps.

When I was nearly at the car I saw three large bonefish working the shoreline no more than twenty feet off the beach in mere inches of water, clearly visible because of the sun's position and the whiteness of the sand bottom. In rough, windy conditions like these, bonefish tend to be less cautious. Still, I knew I would probably have only one cast. Positioning myself so that the backcast would clear overhanging trees, I stripped fly line onto the beach and then delivered a Crazy Charlie to the middle of the three fish. They all rushed the fly, and the biggest one got it. What followed was the longest run I have ever experienced. I was using an old Marryat MR9 reel that held 350 yards of backing, so I was not worried about being stripped. At first, that is. The flat at this point was only a couple of hundred yards wide, and then there was the ultramarine of deep water. The fish reached that in a searing dash and didn't slow up until an honest 250-plus yards of backing were gone. Three more big runs followed. It took the better part of twenty minutes to land and release him. If I had been using a smaller-capacity reel, that fish would have simply spooled me and kept going.

Bonefish become exceedingly wary when subjected to heavy angling pressure. The large, highly educated fish of the Florida Keys, for

Everett hooked up in ankle-deep water.

93

instance, are notoriously difficult to fool with a fly. They have seen every pattern and learned to ignore most of them. On the other hand, there are remote parts of the Bahamas where smaller bonefish have seldom if ever seen a fly and are much easier to hook than their Florida cousins.

Once I was able to fish a small flat that no one had visited for several months, and for the first few days every fish I cast to ate my fly. After that, however, the fish became increasingly nervous, and my success ratio dropped dramatically day by day. On the final morning on a low rising tide I stalked one school after another of tailers flashing in the early sunlight, and they moved just fast enough to stay out of casting range, a maneuver known as a slow spook. When I did manage to get close enough, a good cast would result in a frantic, explosive exit by the entire school. Another school was spooked by a pair of shrilling oystercatchers that flew over them.

Finally I moved to the far end of the flat and stood absolutely still for fifteen minutes, absorbing the colors and the day's lovely promises, scanning the turtlegrass, watching box fish and small sharks swim by, and trying to imitate the statuelike stealth of the great blue heron a hundred yards away. A delicate water sound drew my eye into the light and to two tails only thirty feet away. These were happy fish, feeding intently, not nervous, and both coming to me. Crouching to minimize my silhouette, I managed to cast a pink puff in front of the lead fish. The same cast would have terrorized the earlier schools, but now the vibes had changed. The fish accelerated, tipped, and was on. And then there was that classic hell-bent, furious run. And then another. And a third. And after a while I reached down and grasped the fly and slipped it out of his mouth and watched him regain his strength and move away until his disguise made him invisible again. I felt as though I were part of a timeless ritual that spoke eloquently to a fundamental yearning for contact with our watery beginnings. ◆

Afternoon Sun, Eleuthera oil on paper 9 x 12 inches 2011

"Fly rods," my muse has whispered, "unreel the most direct lifelines to the soul." —Rose Styron, Poet